THE**AMERICANA**
GUITAR**BOOK**

A Complete Guide to Americana Guitar Style & Technique with Stuart Ryan

STUART**RYAN**

FUNDAMENTAL**CHANGES**

The Americana Guitar Book

A Complete Guide to Americana Guitar Style & Technique with Stuart Ryan

ISBN: 978-1-78933-202-5

Published by **www.fundamental-changes.com**

www.fundamental-changes.com

Twitter: @guitar_joseph

Over 11,000 fans on Facebook: **FundamentalChangesInGuitar**

Instagram: **FundamentalChanges**

For over 350 Free Guitar Lessons with Videos Check Out

www.fundamental-changes.com

Cover Image Copyright: Shutterstock / Unsplash

Contents

Introduction

Americana is the name that has been given to the crossroads where Country, Blues, Folk and Bluegrass collide – a century-old musical melting pot that is still developing and evolving. Originally this music was performed on banjos, fiddles and mandolins with the guitar arriving later. The earliest known guitarists in this style were those pioneering the Country music sound: Hank Williams and mandolin pioneer Bill Monroe. Americana came into its own via artists like Woody Guthrie, Pete Seeger, Elizabeth Cotten and The Carter Family, all of whom blended Country, Blues and Folk to create what we now think of as Americana – long before superstars like Bob Dylan and Johnny Cash made it their own. Over the decades the sound of Americana has been shaped by myriad practitioners from the hard-edged sound of Steve Earle to the potent lyricism of today's Americana heroes like Jason Isbell, Chris Stapleton and Lucinda Williams.

Studying Americana will introduce you to many great techniques and approaches that can be applied to both acoustic and electric guitar – from techniques like Travis and Carter picking to slide and raucous electric guitar work. Americana can change how you view the guitar too, opening up the possibility of new textures and rich sounding chords created by various open tunings.

If you are new to this genre, it's a good idea to start by listening to the contemporary (and arguably more accessible) music currently labelled "Americana", played by stars like Alison Krauss and Union Station, Bruce Springsteen, the aforementioned Jason Isbell, and bands like Calexico and Wilco, who have modernised the style while keeping its traditional heart. From here you can explore the timeline that started with the great musicians from the Country and Bluegrass tradition from where Americana was born: Bill Monroe, Hank Williams, Johnny Cash et al.

Because of its fusion of Bluegrass, Country, Folk, traditional Blues and Cajun music, Americana is a window to so many other styles – each of which offers us opportunities for development as guitar players. I trust that you will gain a lot from exploring the different techniques and licks on offer here. The book is organised with a chronological approach, so that you get a sense of how, and from where, Americana has evolved. This will also help you to focus on techniques during the era they were conceived and see how they have developed.

Stuart Ryan

March 2020

Get the Audio

The audio files for this book are available to download for free from **www.fundamental-changes.com.** The link is in the top right-hand corner. Simply select this book title from the drop-down menu and follow the instructions to get the audio.

We recommend that you download the files directly to your computer, not to your tablet, and extract them there before adding them to your media library. You can then put them on your tablet, iPod or burn them to CD. On the download page there is a help PDF and we also provide technical support via the contact form.

For over 350 Free Guitar Lessons with Videos Check out:

www.fundamental-changes.com

Over 11,000 fans on Facebook: **FundamentalChangesInGuitar**

Instagram: **FundamentalChanges**

Chapter One: Essential Techniques

Before we look in depth at the styles of different artists, we have some work to do on the core techniques of Americana, with an initial focus on acoustic guitar. Of particular interest are the techniques developed by certain players that came to bear their names, such as Carter picking and Travis picking.

Carter picking was developed by Maybelle Carter of the famous Carter family. This technique features a combination of picking/brushing that is ideal for self-accompaniment.

Travis picking was developed by the great American fingerpicker Merle Travis and his style exerted a huge influence on a generation of pickers within the Country music world and beyond. Artists like Chet Atkins, Jerry Reed and Tommy Emmanuel took this technique, developed it further and made it their own.

After completing this chapter your picking hand will have received a thorough workout and you'll be familiar with the essential techniques needed for the studies you'll encounter in the rest of this book.

At the turn of the twentieth century, the guitar in Americana would have initially served as an accompaniment instrument, so first of all we will examine the contrasting techniques of strumming and fingerpicking.

In Bluegrass and Appalachian settings, fiddles and mandolins would play the melody of a tune and the guitar would provide backup (having been preceded by the banjo). Example 1a demonstrates an early strumming pattern that alternates between a picked bass note and a strummed chord. The job of the guitar player was to create the illusion of a bass player being present and this simple tactic would do the job! The main challenge here is to achieve good separation between the bass note and strummed chord, so there is independence between the two parts.

Example 1a

The simple bass/chord approach can be developed by adding simple embellishments and bass runs to the sequence. This is great for connecting chords together and it later became a mainstay of Johnny Cash's rhythm style. This example uses a simple hammer-on to break things up and add some movement to the rhythm. Use your second finger for the hammer-on, so that you don't release the full E Major chord shape each time. Instead of a 1, 2, 3, 4 rhythm pattern, notice here how the embellishment in bar 1 results in a count of 1, 2, 3 & 4 which adds more pace and urgency.

Example 1b

Now that you are familiar with the concept of alternating basslines against strumming patterns you can apply the technique to any chord, progression or key. This example uses an A Major chord with the bassline moving from a higher note (the open 5th string) to a lower note (the open 6th string). This is a root to 5th movement (A to E), which is a common progression in Country and Americana accompaniment.

Example 1c

Next, a simple embellishment is added to the bassline, this time with the focus being on the A Major chord. To build these embellishments, aim to land on a chord tone (root, third or fifth) typically from a note just above or below. When this style was being developed the players wouldn't have had theory at the forefront of their minds, it was simply a process of discovering which hammer-on and pull-off patterns sounded good!

Example 1d

Beyond entertaining people, early Americana music was used to dance to – so, in addition to 4/4 time signature, other meters were used. Example 1e takes the concept of the previous examples and applies it to a 3/4 time waltz. Count 1, 2, 3 for each bar and you'll recognise the sound often heard in early Country music by Hank Williams and others. The most common approach for this time signature is a bass/strumming pattern with a slight emphasis on beat 1. Play the bass notes with downstrokes all the way.

Example 1e

The next example is in 3/4 time again, so work on getting that 1, 2, 3 rhythm in place. This one uses a D Major chord and has an alternating root to 5th pattern on the bass – an open D string (root) followed by an open A string (5th). Again, concentrate on accuracy and make sure there is a clear distinction between the open string and the chord. In the audio example you'll also hear a contrast between the bass note and the chord – think loud then quiet.

Example 1f

Fingerpicking is another technique at the core of Americana. There are many different techniques to learn, which would warrant a book in its own right, but here we'll cover some essentials. Early American Folk scene artists like Pete Seeger and Woody Guthrie used fingerstyle techniques extensively and, in turn, influenced the next generation of players like Bob Dylan and Paul Simon, who took Folk Americana into the mainstream.

The following exercise is a simple accompaniment pattern to get you playing some basic fingerstyle. Maintain my suggested picking pattern throughout. We are sticking to the widely used *pima* picking approach. *Pima* is an acronym borrowed from Classical guitar technique, so the names are in Spanish:

p = pulgar (thumb)

i = indice (index finger)

m = medio (middle finger)

a = anular (ring finger)

The thumb (p) normally takes care of the bass notes on strings 6, 5 and 4. The index finger (i) is assigned to string 3, the middle finger (m) to string 2, and the ring finger (a) to string 1. These patterns do occasionally change, but if you're new to fingerstyle it's best to get started by sticking to these finger/string assignments. Take it slowly at first and focus on executing this example as cleanly as possible. Take as much time as you need to train your fingers.

Example 1g

In the next example the bass notes are played against notes located on strings 3, 2 and 1 for a more open sound. This style of playing can naturally develop into instrumental fingerstyle guitar and you'll hear Paul Simon perform some complex solo fingerstyle pieces on recordings from early on in his career.

Example 1h

As the guitar naturally took over from the banjo in early Americana and Folk styles it became more of an accompaniment tool to the voice. Creating the illusion of there being more than one instrument playing was important, so the alternating bassline/strumming technique we've already seen became a huge part of fingerstyle guitar too. The bass movements are commonly the same as we've already seen – root to 5th – and this is demonstrated in the next example. Start slowly with the picking hand fingers so that you get used to the pattern.

Example 1i

An alternating bass/picking pattern thickens the sound considerably by combining the bass notes with the melody on higher strings (i.e. strings 3, 2 and 1). This fuller sound allowed artists from the early American Folk scene to perform with just their voice and guitar. Artists like Bob Dylan and Paul Simon were particularly known for this approach and it meant they were able to tour the country easily and quickly without a large band to rehearse and pay for!

Example 1j

Beyond the basic patterns you've now studied there are other techniques that require you to adapt and change fingerings/patterns. One such technique is "Carter picking", developed by Maybelle Carter of the famous Carter Family. This style owes more to traditional banjo playing. Rather than using the typical *pima* picking finger combinations, Carter would pluck a note with the thumb (usually a bass note, though she would also go as far as string 3), then follow it with an index finger "flick" to sound a chord. When playing Example 1k, stay relaxed. The index finger is do little more than *brushing* the higher strings in order to sound them.

Example 1k

This second Carter picking example develops the technique further. Here there are some typical Carter-style embellishments with hammer-ons to string 4. Notice that the down/up index finger brush/flick technique makes you play on and off the beat. This sound may be familiar to us these days, but it's hard to overstate the influence the artists who developed these techniques had on future generations of players. We have to ask ourselves the question, "How many artists have had a technique named after them?"!

Example 1l

In this example the thumb has a more detailed role and plays simple bass runs in bars two and four. These types of connecting lines were a mainstay of her style and used in both intros and general accompaniment patterns to fill in the role of a bassist. Listen to her classic 'Wildwood Flower' and you'll hear all these elements at play.

Example 1m

Here's one more example of how Maybelle Carter would use bass runs to connect chords e.g. bar 3 going into bar 4. The index finger flick approach is actually quite arbitrary. Although there are times when I've indicated to brush just strings 1 and 2, it won't matter if you catch string 3 as well. Total precision with the index finger is not an essential element of this style.

Example 1n

Merle Travis was another early fingerpicking pioneer. "Travis picking" allows for two independent parts to be picked simultaneously. A simple alternating bassline is usually played on strings 6 and 5, or 6 and 4, then a separate melody line is played over the top on the higher strings. When executed well it gives the impression of two guitarists playing together.

To get started with this technique, you'll first want to practice slightly muting the bass strings. Place the heel of the picking hand (the soft, fleshy part you'd karate chop with!) on the saddle, so it's just resting on strings 6, 5 and 4. Think of it as a "half palm mute". For Travis picking we want the bass strings slightly deadened, while strings 3, 2 and 1 ring out as normal. It helps to create the illusion of a bass player and guitarist working together.

Try playing the simple alternating bassline in Example 1o with the picking hand thumb, making sure that the notes are muted all the way through. Many Travis pickers will use a thumbpick rather than the flesh of their thumb, which gives a crisper, more even attack – but either approach will work. Here there are two basic versions of the Travis picking bassline: the first time around pick string 6 then 4; the second time, hit strings 4 and 3 together. The second pattern is more typical of Merle Travis, while Chet Atkins more often played the first pattern.

Example 1o

12

Example 1p demonstrates another version of the Travis picking bassline. The previous example was a root – octave pattern (strings 6 and 4). This pattern is root – 5th – 5th an octave below (strings 5, 4 and 6 respectively). This pattern is just as common, so spend as much time as you can on this and the previous example before progressing.

Example 1p

In the next example there is more movement in the top line melody while the bassline plays a root – octave pattern. Travis himself had an unusual technique which involved him using just his picking hand thumb and index finger for plucking everything. While die-hard Travis fans will play like this, most guitarists add the middle and ring fingers for picking duties. Chet Atkins is a great example of a player who refined Travis picking to make the technique his own.

Example 1q

Now you can try the other style of bassline while a melody moves over the top. Remember that when Travis picking you are still generally playing through a chord progression, so the thumb must become adept at quickly changing its plucking pattern as the chords change. As you go further into the style, Travis picking will also call for leaving the safe open position and exploring the whole neck, but for now, remaining in open position with minimal fretting hand movement will enable you to focus primarily on the picking hand.

Example 1r

The final example in this chapter will sharpen your ability to move between two different chord shapes and basslines while sustaining a melody line over the top. At first this may feel like a lot to process, so start very slowly and focus on training your thumb to the point where it automatically and accurately plays the bassline.

Example 1s

Chapter Two: The Pioneers

In its earliest form Americana music meant Appalachian mountain music, which gradually developed into a number of different genres from Bluegrass to American Folk. The latter gave voice to artists like Paul Simon, who brought the sound of Americana to a wider audience. However, it also encompassed elements of Country, Blues and Cajun music, which is what makes the term Americana so interesting. It's a catch-all for several different styles and so means different things to different people.

One of the most interesting aspects of its heritage is that it was also heavily influenced by the traditional music of the British Isles, which early settlers took over with them. So, traditional Irish, Scottish and English Folk music is also, ironically, part of the melting pot of this most American of sounds.

In this chapter we'll explore the styles of the early artists who began to define the genre. Some, like Hank Williams, belong firmly to a specific genre such as Country, but nevertheless the influence of such pioneers has been felt far and wide on the generations that followed. Early Blues and Traditional American Folk are also styles you'll explore via artists like Elizabeth Cotten and Maybelle Carter. Finally, you'll dip your toe into the world of Bluegrass with some studies in the style of guitar legends Lester Flatt, Clarence White and Tony Rice.

This first example is based around the accompaniment style of Bluegrass ace Lester Flatt, best known as half of the legendary Flatt and Scruggs, alongside banjo player Earl Scruggs. This is a simple alternating bassline on a D Major chord. Bear in mind that Flatt used a thumbpick, which gave him a different angle of attack and therefore a slightly different sound to a standard pick. Play this with downstrokes all the way.

Example 2a

Example 2b introduces the percussive element of Lester Flatt's style. The D chord is played staccato, which means it only sounds briefly. To achieve this, release the downward pressure from the fretting chord as soon as you've played it, but don't remove the fingers from the strings altogether. Relax and ease off and you'll notice that the chord stops sounding, which gives the initial attack more of a percussive quality. It's akin to the sound a mandolin makes when playing "chop chords" in Bluegrass music.

Example 2b

There is more strumming in this next example. Here the chord is played on beat 2 and its offbeat, as well as beat 4 and its offbeat. If using a thumbpick the approach is similar to the Carter pick/flick style, though here you can use just the picking hand index finger for the down/up flick, or the index, middle and ring fingers together for the down/up motion. Keep it all relaxed; start with a loose wrist and this will stop the fingers from tensing up. This can played with a pick instead of a thumbpick, so try both approaches.

Example 2c

Intros and outros are a huge part of what the guitar does in Bluegrass and Flatt was famed for his "G Major runs" like this one. It's based around a G Major scale in the open position and takes us from G to D and back again. If you only know one Bluegrass lick, this is the one! You may find this easier to play with a plectrum.

Example 2d

16

Hank Williams, the original "Outlaw Country", used the guitar as an accompaniment tool and though his style was simple, he played with great feel and swing which, combined with his choppy style of strumming, captured the rhythm style that is the core of Country playing. This example in 3/4 time shows how an alternating bassline works on a mid-tempo waltz.

Example 2e

The next Hank Williams style example shows how he'd play loose strumming patterns in 4/4 with the alternating bassline approach. Again, note the slight swing feel here and make sure you are accurate when picking the bass notes then chords.

Example 2f

Williams also hinted at the Bluegrass approach in his more up-tempo tracks. The alternating bassline/chord pattern is still here, but the tempo is faster so work on achieving a clean separation between bass and chords. Check that you are playing loosely enough by seeing if you can maintain the stamina to play this pattern over and over again for a few minutes, as you would in a performance.

Example 2g

Elizabeth Cotten was another pioneer of traditional American Folk. Replicating her style is challenging! She was left-handed but, like Jimi Hendrix, played a right-handed guitar upside down. So, when Cotten plucked the bass strings (6, 5, 4) she used her index, middle and ring fingers, and played melodies on strings 3, 2 and 1 with her picking hand thumb. This created a full-sounding accompaniment over which she often sang as well. Cotten frequently used C and G chord shapes, so this is a great way to get accustomed to her style before approaching her pieces.

Example 2h

Open tunings lay at the heart of Cotten's "Country Blues" sound, which influenced so many future singer-songwriters in the Americana genre. This example is in open D Major (from string 6 to 1 tune your guitar D A D F# A D). The open D notes on strings 6 and 4 hark back to the Travis picking alternating bassline approach studied earlier. The picking hand thumb plays the bassline, but note that unlike Travis, Cotten did not mute the bass notes, instead letting them ring out against the melody.

Example 2i

Open D Tuning (DADF#AD)

This example follows on from the previous exercise but uses open G Major tuning (tune to D G D G B D) – another Cotten favourite. When playing in Open G, typically the songs played are in the key of G Major, so string 5 (tuned down to G) is used as the root, while strings 6 and 4 (both tuned to D) are the 5th. There are many ways you can approach playing basslines here, but having this strong root – 5th relationship makes this a very useful tuning to work in.

Example 2j

Open G Tuning (DGDGBD)

Example 2k re-visits the style of Maybelle Carter, but uses a capo higher at the 7th fret to replicate her sound more accurately. Focus on that relaxed thumb/finger interplay and the gentle brushing motion of the picking hand index finger on strings 3, 2 and 1. The hammer-ons and pull-offs need to be as strong as the picked/ brushed notes and, crucially, make sure that the legato phrases aren't rushed or pushed.

Example 2k

Pete Seeger was a legend of the early American Folk scene and spent much of his time playing old time banjo. His background made him an interesting guitarist as he was able to translate some banjo techniques onto guitar. Seeger was a deft fingerpicker who often played 12-string guitar, but this example will stay with 6!

There is a more challenging fingerpicking approach here – the alternating bassline on strings 6 and 4 is still there, but now there is a more complex melody to play over the top.

Example 21

Drop D Tuning (6=D)

Pete Seeger's accompaniment parts weren't all about complexity though. This example shows how he would take a nuanced approach to self-accompaniment on guitar. Note the connecting lines that are used to get from one chord to another – a technique you'll see more of in the guitar style of Johnny Cash.

Example 2m

Chet Atkins was a true pioneer of guitar. At the heart of his approach was the palm-muted, alternating Travis style bassline, but he played complex melodies over the top and drew influence from a wide range of music including Country, Blues, Jazz and beyond. He also arranged well-known pieces for solo guitar and became a superstar in the process. This example features more advanced chord ideas than previous examples, with a melody played over the top. Get your fretting used to what's going on before turning your attention to the picking hand. In bars two and three you will need to use the fretting hand thumb to hold down the first, then second fret of the sixth string as Chet Atkins would do.

Example 2n

Atkins was also adept at playing moving basslines in his music and went beyond the approach of confining the bass notes to the lowest strings. This example shows how a bassline can move around even within the Travis picking style of playing. This is a more complex idea and it may take some time to master, but stick with it as you are truly on the way to sounding like two instruments playing together.

Example 2o

This chapter concludes with the styles of some Bluegrass luminaries. We begin with Clarence White, a member of The Byrds and a Bluegrass legend. This example demonstrates his "crosspicking" rhythm style. Here we return to using a plectrum, so maintain a loose picking hand wrist and relaxed grip.

Example 2p

Clarence White's solos are fantastic. This example highlights the kind of thing he'd play over a typical bluegrass chord progression. Alternate picking is a good approach when playing through parts like this. Aim for the down/up/down/up approach, but remember: it's crucial that the picking and fretting hands are synchronised when playing more challenging parts like these. Learn the fretting hand parts first then build up the picking speed.

Example 2q

Tony Rice may be a new name to you but he's one of the most important guitarists in Bluegrass. Like Chet Atkins, he drew influence from many different genres. You'll obviously hear Bluegrass in his playing, but also plenty of Jazz, Gospel and Blues-inspired ideas. This example is based on the crosspicking technique, arpeggiating chord shapes with some hammer-ons and pull-offs. Relaxation is the key to getting the picking hand working here.

Example 2r

Tony Rice is a superb Bluegrass soloist with impeccable picking technique but also a wealth of musical influences to draw from. He can play at high tempos so this line is challenging but really demonstrates his Bluegrass vocabulary. Based around the G Minor Pentatonic scale, G Blues scale and G Major Pentatonic this needs to be alternate picked apart from the legato techniques suggested.

Example 2s

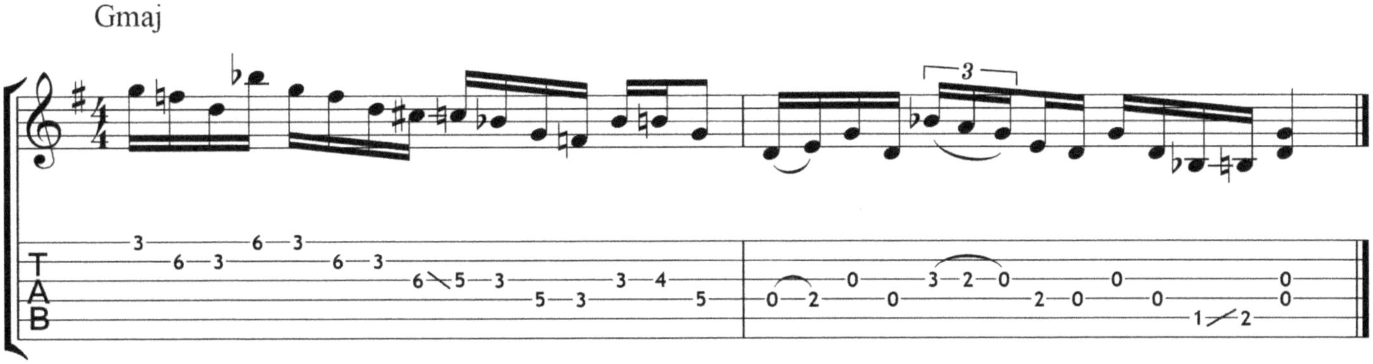

Chapter Three: The Renegades

As America changed, so too did the sound of its music. Hank Williams was perhaps the first Country "outlaw", then other artists began to adopt a harder sound that would emerge as Americana in the decades that followed. Country stars like Johnny Cash didn't hold back from expressing some harsh truths and protest singers like Woody Guthrie brought a harder lyrical edge to the Folk genre. You can hear this influence decades later in the music of artists like Bruce Springsteen and Steve Earle.

This chapter will focus on how Americana emerged as a genre, as artists began fusing together styles like Country, Blues and Folk, which had existed in their own spaces before. As we explore this music further, we will still focus on fundamental techniques like fingerpicking and strumming, but in this era of Americana many bands emerged and the guitar began to come to the fore as a lead instrument. Players like Johnny Cash's sideman Luther Perkins introduced guitar solos, while Bob Dylan rocked the music world by going from acoustic to electric music with The Band.

Woody Guthrie's detailed, complex fingerpicking influenced Paul Simon in particular. Here's an example of his style. The picking hand thumb is doing a lot of work to sound bass notes against static chords. Start off by becoming familiar with the movement within the chord shape, so you can see how the picking and fretting hands interact.

Example 3a

This slower example is an arpeggiated pattern that Guthrie often used. This will do wonders for your picking hand, especially if you are new to fingerpicking. The main challenge is to not rush through this pattern and make sure that you keep the rhythm steady throughout.

Example 3b

Unlike Chet Atkins and Merle Travis, Guthrie would often play melodies in the lower register, on the bass strings. In Example 3c, play the low melody and brush the static chord on strings 3, 2 and 1. Notice the hammer-on and pull-off embellishments that are a hallmark of his style.

Example 3c

As we saw earlier, there are times when we need to play a 3/4 time waltz in Americana. This example shows how Woody Guthrie would play with a mid-tempo waltz feel. This may take some adjusting to, especially for the picking hand, so make sure you are really feeling that 3/4 pulse and don't forget to place a slight emphasis on beat one at the start of each bar.

Example 3d

Johnny Cash's rhythm guitar work propelled his music with pace and swagger. He often strummed muted strings to produce a percussive sound. To do this, hold down a chord then release all downward pressure, so the fingers are resting over the strings. In this example, a bass note is picked followed by muted chord strums. Don't be afraid to totally deaden the strings, that's the objective here.

Example 3e

Amaj   Amaj/E

This uptempo example shows a typical rhythm part Johnny Cash would strum while Luther Perkins played bass melodies or lead parts over the top. The key thing here is to play with a relaxed feel, but still keep the music really tight. Your rhythm playing needs to be in time and each chord strum should last for the same duration. It's actually a lot more precise than it first appears!

Example 3f

Amaj   Amaj/E Dmaj   Dmaj/A   Emaj   Emaj/B   Amaj

Luther Perkins was one of the pioneers of electric and lead guitar in Country music and his "twangy" sound can be heard across later Americana. This example features the type of simple accompaniment idea he would play – a arpeggiated chord picked with light palm muting. Try adding some slapback delay to your sound for maximum authenticity!

Example 3g

Example 3h features the type of melodic part Luther Perkins would play on intros and outros. Again, note the twang factor achieved by playing parts like this on the bass strings. Aim for a clean electric tone here. You don't want any hint of distortion to get this to sounding right.

Example 3h

Perkins elevated the role of the guitar from a rhythm to a lead instrument, and while Americana is not a genre fixated with virtuoso lead lines, there are plenty of impresive breaks and solos to learn. This is a Perkins style lead line that focuses on developing a melody rather than just noodling around the fretboard.

Example 3i

Bob Dylan, perhaps the best known of all American Folk artists, became a superstar and, in the process, took many of Americana's traits into mainstream music. Influenced by Woody Guthrie, you'll hear many of the same approaches in his playing but also some more colourful chordal ideas like in this example.

Example 3j

This example revisits the open D Major tuning seen earlier in the Elizabeth Cotten example. When working in open tunings you'll often find that the tuning itself does a lot of the work for you – meaning less effort for the fretting hand. It's easy to create melodic parts that sound more complex than they are!

Example 3k

Open D Major Tuning (DADF#AD)

Dylan often strums rhythm parts too, especially when playing in a full band context where his guitar is not the primary focus. This rhythm pattern contrasts simple "1, 2, 3, 4" rhythms with more challenging "1 e & a, 2 e & a, 3 e & a, 4 e & a" patterns. This type of playing is all about being loose and relaxed. If you're not relaxed, the faster phrases won't fall into place.

Example 3l

Here's another example of Dylan's strumming style – an approach that would shape the accompaniment ideas of generations of Americana guitarists. It's all here: moving bass notes, strummed chords and hammer-on and pull-off embellishments.

Example 3m

To get Dylan's style in place you need to be comfortable with uptempo fingerpicking and quick chord changes. Example 3n features both and demands quick movement on both picking and fretting hands. Again, you can hear how this is a development from the earlier Woody Guthrie sound. The fingerpicking is more rapid and there is more colour, thanks to the use of faster chord changes and more colorful chords like dominant 7ths.

Example 3n

Example 3o

Playing in 3/4 time is a skill to constantly develop and Dylan was a master at playing with a "chunky" rhytmic feel. For this next example you need to get a strong attack on beat one, followed by a lighter strum on the chord on the higher strings. Get those dynamics right and you'll really hear the 3/4 waltz feel come through.

The layering of acoustic and electric guitars is a key feature of Americana guitar. When Dylan incorporated electric guitars into his band he created the template for this approach. Here, a simple strummed acoustic guitar pattern creates the foundation for the following example.

Example 3p

This example overlays an electric guitar part onto the previous example. This approach is about keeping out of the way of the busy strummed acoustic guitar, which is done by keeping the rhythms simple, the part melodic (chord arpeggios are used to outline the progression) and in a higher register, so as to not clash with the acoustic part.

Example 3q

In this and the next two examples you'll see how you can overlay two electric parts over an acoustic foundation. In the first example an acoustic guitar simply strums the underlying chord progression with a 1, 2, 3, 4 rhythm. The acoustic is not meant to be the focus of the track here, so the straightforward strumming approach works well.

Example 3r

Now an electric riff-based idea is added to the track, which starts to give it more cohesion and interest. In order to play the chords, make sure you use the index finger to barre across the fifth fret and the ring/third finger to barre across the seventh fret. For the final chord in bar one, use the index finger barred across the fifth fret and the middle/second finger for the note on the sixth fret.

Example 3s

Finally, some electric licks are added. Remember, in Americana it's more about what serves the track than individual virtuosity, so ideas like this are typically melodic and restrained.

Example 3t

Townes Van Zandt is one of the most important figures in the development of Americana and his influence still resonates today. Influenced by Bob Dylan, his fingerpicking parts can be quite complex and also go beyond simple major and minor sounds, sometimes containing unexpected tension and release as in this example.

Example 3u

This second Townes Van Zandt inspired example shows how he embellishes simple chord progressions to create a style and sound that is at the very core of Americana guitar. This is another example of how a solid, consistent bassline underpins a simple melody over the top. Remember, this is all about keeping the picking hand thumb independent while the fingers sound the melody over the top. Coordination is the hard thing with this style!

Example 3v

Chapter Four: The Hitmakers

The term "Americana" was not actually coined until the early 1980s, even though the music that led to the creation of the genre had been around much longer. As time went on, Bluegrass, Country Blues and Traditional Folk music remained niche styles, while Country and early Rock became mainstream concerns. We've already seen how Bob Dylan combined Folk and Blues guitar techniques with his lyrical song writing skills to become a huge star and pioneer of the early Americana sound. In this chapter we'll look at more artists who became household names and see how they used the guitar to move the genre along. The 1960s and 70s saw some of the world's great music stars emerge – artists like Paul Simon, Neil Young, Tom Petty and Bruce Springsteen. While each had their own strong identity, they often drew from the same pool of influences discussed in previous chapters.

The development of the electric guitar in the 1950s undoubtedly shaped the sound of Americana and while acoustic guitar remains at the forefront of the style, electric guitar parts were used to add their own unique character from this point onwards.

In this chapter you'll learn more fingerpicking techniques and see how the style has continued to develop. You'll also learn how to play guitar with a chunky attack, and how to create characteristic jangly guitar parts. Artists like Woody Guthrie and Elizabeth Cotton often worked in a solo context, but the generation that followed them often played in a band setting, which meant two or even three guitarists working together. For that reason, we'll spend more time focusing on how to layer guitar parts so that they intertwine, without getting in each other's way.

Country Star Emmylou Harris is an example of how a singer-songwriter can create melodic guitar parts that complement the vocal and song perfectly. This fingerpicked example features a melody played from within a chord shape – a common tool for artists in Country and Americana genres. The key here is balance: don't let any part ring out louder than another.

Example 4a

Gmaj   Gsus4   Cmaj   Gmaj

Paul Simon is one of the most famous names in Pop music history and his work, both solo and as one half of Simon and Garfunkel, brought the American Folk sound well into the mainstream. Simon's fingerpicking style can be traced back to Woody Guthrie and even earlier. Simon's uptempo picking and strumming patterns are a great way to hone your technique. This example hints at both Blues and Rock 'n' Roll.

Example 4b

Dmaj   E7   Gmaj   Dmaj

This next example demonstrates how Paul Simon brought a more modern approach to the Folk genre by using chords with more colour. Here we have the sound of Add11 and Add9 chords, which makes things sound more melodic than simple major and minor chords. This part can be fingerpicked on acoustic or played with a pick on electric.

Example 4c

Amaj   Asus2   Asus4

Example 4d demontrates several quintessential Paul Simon ideas within just a few bars – from the hammer-on chord of G Major to C in the first bar to the classic alternating bassline on the C Major chord – this is pure Simon. Add in the D Major chord with just a touch of colour from the open 2nd string (which creates a D Major 6 sound) and there is plenty to work on! Use the third finger to hold down fret three of string 6 and the index and middle fingers to sound the hammer-ons on strings 2 and 4 respectively.

Example 4d

Gmaj   Cmaj/G   Gmaj   Dmaj/F#   Cmaj   Gmaj   Cmaj/G   Gmaj

Neil Young is one of the true pioneers of Americana. His output ranges from pastoral acoustic folk to blistering electric guitar via his work with Crazy Horse. His impact on the world of Americana is undeniable and the wide range of his style is essential learning for anyone interested in the genre. From his work with Crosby, Stills, Nash and Young, as a soloist, with Buffalo Springfield and Crazy Horse, he is perhaps the text book definition of Americana.

To get Young's strumming technique right you have to palm mute the low notes of these chords with a heavy down strum then quickly release the mute to catch the higher strings un-muted. It's not easy but this is what creates the chunky rhythm sound he is famous for.

Example 4e

Young's tonal and textural approach to acoustic playing/writing is very detailed and gives way to a more modern way of writing Americana and Folk. This example demonstrates how he will move out of the open position to create tense, dark minor chords, before moving back to a major tonality with a more typical singer-songwriter approach to the instrument.

Example 4f

Here is another example of how Young will move out of the open position to get more open strings and consequently more unique sounding chords into his writing. This one is played with a swing feel so make sure you are relaxed all the way through and aim for his characteristic heavy downstrum.

Example 4g

Drop D Tuning (6 = D)

Young's output with Crazy Horse is a complete contrast to his acoustic work. Heavy guitars and riff based playing dominate here, along with lead work and the power of drop D tuning (tune string 6 down a tone). This example is a power chord based idea that is typical of his work with the group. Aim for a fuzz-laden tone and a heavy, loose attack when playing in this style.

Example 4h

Drop D Tuning (6 = D)

As with Bob Dylan, artists like Bruce Springsteen took the influence of pioneers like Woody Guthrie and Pete Seeger and made that sound their own. Springsteen is so influenced by Pete Seeger that he recorded a cover album of Seeger's material. Springsteen is a great fingerpicker and strummer with that traditional American sound prevalent in all his acoustic work. This example shows how he will take a slow, measured approach to some strumming parts with just a bit of colour added to each chord.

Example 4i

This example is characterstic of how Springsteen will play through a I-IV-V chord progression. Instead of playing simple major chords, he opts for drop D tuning and plays chords that have more colour, e.g the open 3rd and 1st strings in the D chord. You'll find these ideas time and again in his writing, and these chords will often be picked/fingerpicked (as in this example) or strummed.

Example 4j

Drop D Tuning (6 = D)

Following on from the previous example this exercise expands on the drop D tuning to use another Springsteen favourite, double drop D. Here the first string is tuned down a tone to D as well. It is the combination of this tuning and these chord voicings that creates the huge, explosive rhythm sound that is such a big part of Springsteen's acoustic playing.

Example 4k

Double Drop D tuning (6 = D, 1 = D)

Sticking with the theme of alternate tunings, here's an example influenced by Ry Cooder, a guitarist who has fused together many different styles over the years. Cooder has worked within every genre from Blues to Cajun, Americana and more. He is a true virtuoso with his own distinct voice. This example is in drop D and is a 12-bar blues style rhythm example. This can be played with a pick, but fingers will give you more control over the necessary string separation. Electric or acoustic guitars will work well for an idea like this.

Example 4l

Drop D Tuning (6 = D)

Many of rock legend Tom Petty's approaches and techniques echo the great artists who preceded him. This deft fingerpicking example makes the most of drop D tuning and focuses on an alternating bassline throughout. The key here is independence between the picking hand thumb and fingers. If necessary, just work on alternating strings 6 and 4 with the thumb before adding anything else, as this is all about co-ordination.

Example 4m

Drop D Tuning (6 = D)

This example and the following one show how Tom Petty and Mike Campbell would typically interlock guitar parts. This simple idea uses just open chords, but watch out for the Dsus2 chord played on the "and" of beat four each time.

Example 4n

Mike Campbell is a master of coming up with second guitar parts and this idea is designed to be played over the previous example. Note the constant use of a "pedal note" – a note that is used over and over to act as a "hinge" for the whole part. In this case it's the open 1st string that is the anchor. You can use a lightly overdriven tone for this sort of part, though it will work equally well on acoustic.

Example 4o

Jackson Browne is one of the great American singer-songwriters who is firmly rooted in the Americana tradition. This fingerpicking example is typical of his playing. The picking hand thumb keeps a steady alternating bassline to anchor the beat, while the remaining fingers pluck notes both on and off the beat. This is all about coordination and will be a great exercise if you are working to develop more independence in your picking hand.

Example 4p

James Taylor needs no introduction – a legendary guitarist and songwriter who fuses American Folk, Blues, Pop and Americana into his sound. Melodic acoustic guitar playing is at the core of everything Taylor does and his introductions to pieces are like mini compositions in themselves. In this example, notice how moving triads up and down the neck against a static bass note gives this riff its defining character.

Example 4q

Guitarist Robbie Robertson and The Band in general are one of the main groups who gave birth to the Americana sound. They already had a solid pedigree as Bob Dylan's backing band and when they started writing their own material they furthered the development of Americana with their fusion of Blues, Southern Soul, Country and so much more. This rhythm example relies on playing with a loose feel and a relaxed approach throughout. Start off with a standard E Major chord shape then flatten the third finger across fret two to sound the following chord.

Example 4r

The Eagles are one of the most successful Country Rock groups of all time but they are much more than that, with a wide range of influences that helped shape the nascent Americana sound. This example shows the almost Mexican Mariachi style influence in their writing and playing. Piece this together with the next example and you'll hear how it all takes shape. A rapid down/upstroke is needed to play these parts, so keep the wrist loose and relaxed.

Example 4s

Harmony guitar was a hallmark of The Eagles' sound and this example features two guitars outlining the underlying chord progression with arpeggios to achieve that almost Latin sound that feels like a huge departure from classic Country. This sound would go on to form the bedrock of later bands under the Americana banner, in particular acts like Calexico.

Example 4t

Chapter Five: The Renaissance

As the 1970s drew to a close, a fusion of various styles of music had taken place – some of which had waned, while others had flourished. Although the term "Americana" wasn't recognised until the early 1980s, leading up to this a number of new singer-songwriters were honing their craft. They didn't have the same profile as the well-known acts discussed in previous chapters, but they too were developing their own sound. Over the decades that followed, these new artists would be able to work under the banner of Americana to further shape their sound and find their audience. Their music would contain elements of Country, Blues, Folk and Bluegrass, without strictly adhering to any one style. They would reject the bombast of the bigger, modern Country sound and instead focus on acoustic parts and textural electric guitar to support their song writing. Some, like Steve Earle, would bring a harder edged sound to the genre. Others, like Gillian Welch would work with a softer approach and lyricism.

In this chapter we'll explore the styles of some of the most significant artists from the 1980s onwards. The electric guitar begins to occupy a more prominent role in this music and we'll also examine how the interplay between two guitars is often critical to the genre.

John Hiatt is an artist who has taken Americana into the modern age. His fingerpicking style is a great example of how to drive things along rhythmically. For this example, pluck the bass notes with the picking hand thumb and pluck strings 3, 2 and 1 with the ring, middle and index fingers respectively. Follow this with a downward flick on the same strings with the nails of these fingers, then pluck the strings as before on the "and" of beat 2. Don't forget to play this with a swing feel too!

Example 5a

Gillian Welch is another major presence on today's Americana scene and it could be argued that her work with Dave Rawlings defines the genre. Rich sounding chords and embellished voicings are a hallmark of her style. Play this one with a relaxed feel but make sure the hammer-on embellishments are well timed. The descending bassline/chord run in bar four is classic Country/Americana.

Example 5b

Sidekick to Gillian Welch, Dave Rawling's flowing lead lines add great melodic content to her rhythm playing. Try this idea over the previous example. There are hints of Bluegrass, Blues and Americana in this Rawlings-style lick. Consider how he outlines each chord with some extensions (e.g. Cmaj7 in bar 3) and embellishments.

Example 5c

Steve Earle is a huge figure in the worlds of both Americana and Alt Country. He also has a great range as a writer and player, from stripped back acoustic ballads to heavier, almost rock-inspired work. This example focuses on his melodic acoustic fingerpicking side. This one is all about taking a standard chord progression but making it more interesting by connecting each chord with various licks and embellishments. You can fingerpick this with the standard *pima* picking hand approach you have used so far.

Example 5d

You'll also find an Appalachian/Celtic influence in Earle's playing and writing. This next example shows how he will build melodies into his electric rhythm playing. This is all about notes on one string moving againt a pedal tone (or repeated note, usually an open string). The aim here is to get onto the fingertips of the fretting hand so you can keep the open 3rd string ringing in the first bar.

Example 5e

This example features a classic Americana style chord progression that is used by Gillian Welch and many others. Instead of a simple G Major to C Major move you are playing G Major with various embellishments (the hammer-ons) followed by one of the most common chords in Americana, a Cadd9. This simply means a C Major chord with an added D note (the 9th) placed on the top of the chord. The resulting shape is virtually identical to the G Major chord it follows.

Example 5f

Gmaj   Cadd9   Em   Dmaj   Dsus4/G

Blues fingerpicking is a huge part of Americana and this example is influenced by the great Blues/Roots musician Bonnie Raitt. This examples demonstrates the influence of Skip James on her playing. There are several challenges here: first, the 12/8 time signature which means every beat has a triplet feel ("1 and a 2 and a" etc), and second, you'll need to focus on independence between the picking hand thumb playing the low notes and the melody/lick that's played over the top.

Example 5g

E7#9   Emaj   E5   E6

P.M.--|

Another great contemporary artist working within the Folk/Roots/Americana genre is Melissa Etheridge. This example demonstrates her heavily percussive acoustic rhythm playing. To play the muted strings (those marked with an X) you must release the pressure on the fretting hand fingers before quickly reapplying it to sound the subsequent chord. There's quite a lot of coordination required here, so start slow and build up the speed.

Example 5h

```
        Am7                    Am                    D5      Gmaj    Amaj/E

T —————X—5—X—5—X—5—X—5———X—5—X—5—X—5—X—5———X—3—X—3—X—3———————0————0—2—X—2—X—2—X—2——
A —————X—5—X—5—X—5—X—5———X—7—X—7—X—7—X—7———X—2—X—2—X—2———————0————0—2—X—2—X—2—X—2——
B —————X—0—X—0—X—0—X—0———X—0—X—0—X—0—X—0———X—0—X—0—X—0———————0————0—2—X—2—X—2—X—2——
                                                                    3
```

Lyle Lovett came to prominence in the 1980s and while he is often referred to as a Country artist there are many things in his playing which put him firmly in the Americana camp. This particular example is a bluesy fingerpicking part inspired by Merle Travis and the Delta Greats. Again, it's about separating out what the picking hand thumb is doing (the bass) while playing the melody line over the top with the index and middle or index, middle and ring fingers. Some palm muting on the bass can help with separation here.

Example 5i

```
   Gmaj   G7    Gmaj                D7/A              Gmaj

T ———3————————1——————————3——————0—————————3————————5—————0——————————————
A —————0——————————0————————0———————0———5———————4——————4———————0——————0———
B ———3————————3———————3————————3——————5—————————5————————3——————3————————
     0      0        0       0
```

For many people REM are synonymous with the Americana sound. While their later albums had more of a rock influence, in the early days Americana was certainly a driving part of their sound. Guitarist Peter Buck is definitely a lynchpin within the Americana genre – his parts often melding guitar, mandolin and many other traditional stringed instruments into a track. This part features arpeggiated chords. It can be played fingerstyle but try using a pick to work on your crosspicking technique to jump across the strings.

Example 5j

In this example you are strumming a Peter Buck style chord part in 6/8 time. Think "1 & a 2 & a". Staying within the rhythmic feel is important here as this time signature is very common within the genre, drawing influence from its roots in traditional Irish, Folk and Appalachian styles. A loose, relaxed strumming wrist is critical when playing this kind of part.

Example 5k

Expanding on the previous Peter Buck inspired crosspicking part, this one develops things further. There are some good challenges for you here: firstly maintaining the rhythm and secondly working on that crosspicking technique to jump from string to string. Finally, note the runs that are used to connect each chord at the end of the bar. These are derived from Country and Bluegrass and have become essential features of Americana.

Example 5l

John Mellencamp found fame in the 1980s just as the term Americana was being recognised. Like Bruce Springsteen, his sound often veers towards rock but latterly he has really embraced the Americana label and worked within it. This first example shows how a palm muted acoustic guitar can play simple power chords to capture the sound of the genre. The key thing here are the accents, which fall on the "and" of beats 2 and 4. Listen to the audio and make sure you emphasise these parts so it sounds right.

Example 5m

```
          F5                                        C5                      G5
          >        >           >        >              >        >              >        >
 4
 4

 P.M.- - - - - - - - - - - - - - - - - - - - - - - - - - - - - - - - - - - - - - - - - - - - -|

T
A                                                 5-5—5-5—5-5—5-5
B     3-3—3-3—3-3—3-3    3-3—3-3—3-3—3-3    3-3—3-3—3-3—3-3    5-5—5-5—5-5—5-5
      1-1—1-1—1-1—1-1    1-1—1-1—1-1—1-1                       3-3—3-3—3-3—3-3
```

Being able to layer guitar parts is an essential feature of Americana and this example is designed to sit on top of the previous exercise. The modern sounding Fsus2 and Csus2 chords really help to define the sound of Americana from the 1980s onwards and are well worth committing to memory, as you'll often find them being used within the genre.

Example 5n

```
          Fsus2                              Csus2                    Gmaj
 4
 4

T          ----1----          ----1----
A      ---0----     -0----0--     -0---          -0--            -0---
B    3-         -3-     -3-         -3-     -3-      -0---0--0--    -0-2---0--
                                          3-                -3-  3-      -2-
```

The name John Prine may be new to you but he is one of the old guard of the Americana genre, having emerged in the late 1970s and established himself in the 1980s. Regarded as one of the great songwriters within the genre, his guitar style is steeped in roots and blues. This fingerpicked example features the clasisc alternating bassline approach with a syncopated (off the beat) melody line played over the top. The simple chord shapes won't challenge the fretting hand but there may be work for the picking hand here.

Example 5o

Alison Krauss and Union Station are often referred to as Bluegrass or "Newgrass", but there is a great deal of Americana in the band's approach. Guitarists Dan Tyminski and Ron Block are both superb fingerpickers and flatpickers who also bring a more modern chord sound to the genre. This progression features more advanced, fresh sounding versions of E minor, C Major and D Major chords that contribute to their traditonal-meets-modern approach.

Example 5p

This second Tyminski/Block inspired example again focuses on their chord work. Notice the abundant use of open strings to expand and extend the chords, moving them away from simple major or minor. This reinforces the band's more modern approach and puts a more interesting spin on a well-used chord progression.

Example 5q

Finally, this example shows how a chord sequence can be outlined simply by playing a moving bassline against a static part. This shows how Tyminski and Block will move through a standard chord progression by creating a defined part rather than just strumming the underlying chords. You can play this fingerstyle or with a pick. I'd aim for the latter to best mimic how these guitarists often play. You may also find the pick gives a crisper, more defined sound for a part like this.

Example 5r

Chapter Six: Americana Today

The term Americana was formally included in the Merriam-Webster dictionary in 2011 and defined as "A genre of American music having roots in early folk and country music." As you have seen throughout this book, these early styles are indeed at the core of the genre, but there are now many offshoots from this style.

Terms like Alt Country (mentioned in passing earlier) and Outlaw Country are just some of the sub-sets that have emerged in recent years. What's more important, however, is how the Americana artists of today are defining the genre for themselves. The acoustic guitar remains at the fore, but now there are more complex arrangements that go beyond simple chord progressions. Alongside this is the inclusion of instruments like slide guitar, piano and strings. Distorted eletric guitars are just as likely to sit alongside acoustic fingerpicking and the overall sound of the genre has become heavier and, in some cases, darker.

Today, Americana is often found in mainstream music, be it through its use on TV and film soundtracks or through the huge success of artists like Chris Stapleton who blur the boundaries between Americana, Country and Alt Country. There have been hugely succesful, high profile collaborations within the genre, such as those between Alison Krauss and Led Zeppelin's Robert Plant on their *Raising Sand* album.

In this chapter you'll study the styles and techniques of today's Americana artists. You'll see how the electric guitar starts to play a bigger role and how the current generation have built on the technical foundations you've already explored. Here are fresh sounding chords and, in some cases, a more demanding approach. In addition, you'll see how the guitar is often used as a writing tool to create distinct parts in a song, rather than for simple accompaniment.

In Example 6a, the simple rhythm pattern highlights a common strumming pattern in modern Americana. It features the ubiquitous Cadd9 chord which really evokes the contemporary Americana sound. This is classic singer-songwriter stuff. Check out artists like Lucinda Williams to hear these ideas in action. Aim for a gentle, realaxed strum which is light on the strumming hand. Don't dig in too much at first, so that you leave headroom for when it's needed.

Example 6a

This idea will work well on both acoustic and electric guitar. It's a simple intro or fill in G Major that expands the underlying chord sound. It's well worth having a large supply of similar ideas at the ready. This example works well with the preceding one. Note how the simple chord progression of Example 6a starts to sound more musical and modern when this idea is overlaid.

Example 6b

Chris Isaak appeared on the scene in the 1990s and had several huge chart hits, which well and truly took his brand of Americana into the mainstream. Cinematic in scope, this style of Americana is about dreamy, wistful sounds. Enriching the chords with some simple extensions, as in this example, is a great shortcut to this sound. Listen to how the B and E chords are given more depth than their standard major counterparts.

Example 6c

You can play Example 6d over the previous exercise to hear how things open up even more when an arpeggiated part is played over an interesting chord progression. This one works well on acoustic but will give more of a modern Americana sound if played on electric with some delay and reverb to create a more expansive sound. Let all the notes ring out and try adding extra touches to the part, be it via the whammy bar or effects like tremelo.

Example 6d

Bm add4   Dadd2   Emaj/G#   E13

There are some bands that have come to define the sound of modern Americana and Wilco are one of the most prominent. There have been several line-up changes, but guitarists Jeff Tweedy and Nels Cline understand how the interplay between several guitar parts work. First, try playing this simple chord figure that features a few subtle embellishents and a tweaked C Major voicing.

Example 6e

Am   Am11   Cadd9

Play this idea over the previous example to hear how an arpeggiated guitar part can add depth to a simple two chord progression. There are many approaches you can take tonally here. For a truly modern sound I'd recommend a slightly overdriven electric guitar with a touch of delay and reverb, along with some tremelo set in time to the beat.

Example 6f

Am   Cmaj

Singer-songwriter Aimee Mann is an artist who blurs musical boundaries to create her signature sound. Rock, 1960s Pop and Americana all loom large in her writing. A great rhythm player, she often creates parts like that in Example 6g to connect chords with simple bass runs/riffs. The challenge here is to play the single notes with slight palm muting, followed by a clean open chord to contrast the percussive riffing with strumming. Aim for quite a heavy attack when playing this type of part.

Example 6g

While many of the artists we've encountered so far have modernised the sound of Americana with intertwined guitars and rich chord voicings, there are also plenty who hark back to the traditional sound of simple fingerpicked ideas. This part is inspired by songwriters like Iris DeMent, who used the guitar as a supporting voice with a very traditional sound.

Example 6h

We are back to the more modern style of writing here with a part inspired by singer-songwriter Rodney Crowell. The bright, rich sounding chords take us out of the open position and hint at a more Pop-orientated Americana sound. The important thing here is to get the chord shapes cleanly in place so the strumming hand is doing the work. Note how the use of open strings against chords higher up the neck gives that bright, open sound.

Example 6i

Emaj 6/9   E6sus2   Emaj/A   Esus4   Emaj

Americana has become a huge, wide-ranging genre that also encompasses influences from the worlds of Cajun, Tex-Mex, Mariachi and much more. One band who fuse together multiple genres is Calexico, who create tense, moody soundscapes with intertwining guitar parts. This part can be played on acoustic or electric but pay attention to the 12/8 time signature which splits the beats into triplets and dictates the overall feel.

Example 6j

$\bullet. = 42$

Cmaj   Em

Example 6k is designed to be played on electric guitar and loosely outlines Em and C Major chords to create a slightly tense melodic part. In terms of tone, big reverbs, delay and a driven sound work well to get that modern Indie-Rock/Americana sound you need for this style.

Example 6k

♩. = 42

The next example is inspired by artists like Ray LaMontaigne and Ryan Adams – singer-songwriters who have broken through to the mainstream with a sound that is built upon Americana foundations. You are playing in 6/8 here, so make sure you have the correct rhythmic feel in place and as always aim for that loose, relaxed strumming hand. A good tip for this sort of rhythm is a lighter pick that will bounce off the strings quickly.

Example 6l

As you saw at the start of this book, in the early days of Country and Americana the guitar parts were often quite simple and in support of the voice. These days the guitar parts are often composed and form an integral part of the song itself. Artists like Jason Isbell are adept at creating parts that add an extra hook along with the vocal. This style is partly dependent on the fretting hand being able to move quickly and smoothly between single notes and chords.

Example 6m

Artists like Country superstar Chris Stapleton are adept at writing simple guitar parts that provide the perfect accompaniment. These parts usually feature tight, cohesive rhythms and embellishments like the ones you'll find here. Being able to link chords with short runs like this is an essential part of getting the Americana sound in place, whether you're playing acoustic or electric guitar.

Example 6n

Following on from the previous example here is a short phrase that shows how to connect chords with simple runs. This time though there are "grace notes", such as just before beat 4 at the end of the first bar. Grace notes are an integral part of this style but are quite hard to execute, as they often rely on a very fast hammer-on or pull-off which is sounded only briefly. You'll hear this in the modern Americana playing of bands like Mandolin Orange.

Example 6o

The waltz is a common feel in Americana and this 3/4 example is inspired by the great American guitarist/songwriter/producer Buddy Miller who, along with T Bone-Burnett and WG Snuffy Walden, brought Americana into the mainstream via TV and movie soundtracks. This feel can be difficult if you are new to it, so make sure you are feeling three beats in each bar and watch out for the challenging triplet phrase at the end of bar 1, as this can be difficult to time correctly.

Example 6p

Often Americana artists will break out of simple I-IV-V chord progressions by using moving basslines against chord shapes that remain static on top. This example is influenced by the Avett Brothers and shows the effect a moving bassline can have. The trade off is that the fretting hand needs to be well coordinated and confident, and sometimes you'll have to change fingering mid-performance in order to accommodate the moving bass/static chord idea.

Example 6q

Adding melody and the occasional slight dissonance to a chord progression can help with getting the bittersweet sound that is so prevalent in modern Country and Americana. You'll hear this effect in the playing and writing of artists like Kacey Musgraves. While you can play this example fingerstyle, it really relies on the crosspicking technique where the pick is jumping across the strings.

Example 6r

While much of today's Americana has that wistful, modern sound there are also plenty of artists who hark back to the origins of the style and proudly showcase a sound that is infuenced by tradtional Country and Delta Blues. One such artist is Poky LaFarge and this example shows how he will use the Delta Blues and Swing sound as a writing tool. Play this one fingerstyle and think about how it hints at the first examples you studied in this book.

Example 6s

In the final chapter, I have put together four longer tracks for you to learn, which seek to encompass the breadth of the Americana genre. Each comes with playing guidance and, of course, audio examples so you can hear exactly how they should sound.

Chapter Seven: Americana Study Pieces

Track 1

This jaunty, mid-tempo track in G Major demonstrates how the "old time" sound of Americana gets used in a modern band context. The acoustic guitar drives this track and the parts can be played with a pick or fingerstyle. When playing in this style, the idea is to outline chord progressions with melodic embellishments, so that you don't rely on a simple chord/strum approach. Although we are dealing with the primary chords in the key of G Major – the I (G), IV (C), V (D) and vi (Em) – notice how the embellishments give the rhythm parts far more character. The whole piece starts to sound more like a song than just a strummed or picked chord sequence. There is also a swing feel throughout, so aim to stay relaxed when picking and strumming and try to match the feel of the track.

You'll also explore a wide range of the fretboard in this track, from the high register at the twelfth fret, all the way down to open position. It's common for guitarists in this genre to veer between strumming/embellishments and high melody parts, so it's good to get used to jumping up and down the neck!

The opening lick is based around the G Major Pentatonic scale (G, A, B, D, E) – a staple of Bluegrass and Americana sounds. It's important to get this lick sounding smooth, so a number of legato techniques are employed to facilitate this: hammer-ons, pull-offs and slides are all useful in smoothing this line out. While Bluegrass guitar players aim to alternate pick as much as possible, there are times when you want to reduce the string attack with legato. When you have learned this part, try writing a similar lick of your own using this scale, then practice it against the backing track to see how it sounds.

Some of the phrases may initially feel challenging, for example in bar 15 where you have to jump from string 4 over to string 3. While you can pick this or use fingerstyle technique, also try out the pick and finger hybrid approach we studied earlier in this book. It's tailor made for situations like this.

From bar 17 there are a succession of embellished C chords. These are classic Bluegrass ideas and you'll be able to use them in other scenarios where C is the IV chord. Playing these embellishments adds great melodic content to parts and stops you from just holding on for dear life and strumming chords! Similarly, the ideas in bars 31-32 show how various D chords can be sounded by just using double-stops against an open D string.

Example 7a

Cmaj
C7 C6
G5
17
CMaj
C9
G5
21
Cmaj
C9 C6
Gmaj
Dmaj
24
Em
Cmaj
A7
28

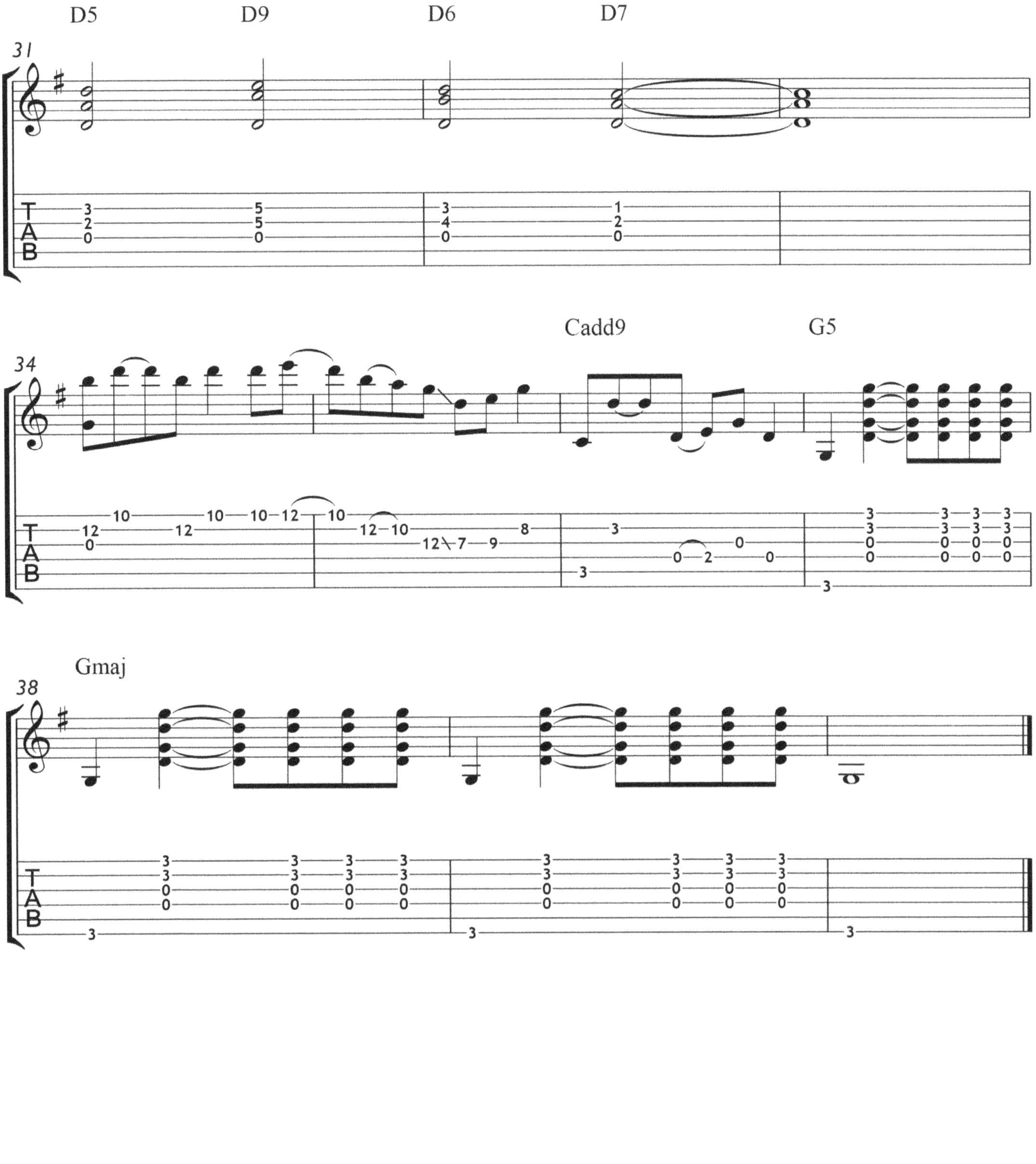
D5
D9
D6
D7
31
Cadd9
G5
34
Gmaj
38

Track 2

The second track is all about fingerpicking. You'll be putting into practice techniques that have been used by everyone from Paul Simon and Bob Dylan to Jason Isbell and beyond. Here you are playing a melodic fingerstyle part – the kind of part that can be used in a full band context, or on its own to accompany a singer.

There are typically two parts to this type of track: first, a repeating, alternating bassline generally played on strings 6 and 4, or 5 and 4 depending on the chord, and second, a melodic figure that sits over the top of the bassline – usually to add interest to the part or it can double up the vocal melody.

The main focus here is developing control and independence over the picking hand thumb and fingers. The thumb plucks the bass notes with a steady 1 & 2 & 3 & 4 & rhythm, while the picking hand fingers pluck the melody lines over the top. The challenge, of course, is that you have two rhythms to play – the solid, repetitive bassline, set against the melody which features a great deal of syncopation (notes that are not played on the beat and sometimes aren't even on the offbeat either!) The beat can be divided into semiquavers, resulting in a count of 1 e & a 2 e & a 3 e & a 4 e & a. The melody can fall on any of these divisions within each beat. It's common for fingerstyle players to add melodies over basslines without giving a second thought to where they fall on the beat but, when you come to play their pieces yourself this can prove especially taxing!

This particular track has been given more of a modern, contemporary feel by using a variety of add9 chords. You've seen these throughout the book and in many ways they define the sound of Americana and modern Country. When you have learned this track, try replacing them with standard major chords. The difference will be quite subtle, but you'll hear how removing the colour of the ninth makes things sound a bit more traditional.

Another common device used by today's players and writers is to add some movement within a chord and you'll see examples of this from bar 14. Simple melodies can be played on the top strings against the steady bassline and this is another way of getting away from just playing the chords. The outro section from bar 29 hints at this modern sound with various chords with colour added. Note that you don't have to play an F Major barre chord when there are so many other options available!

Example 7b

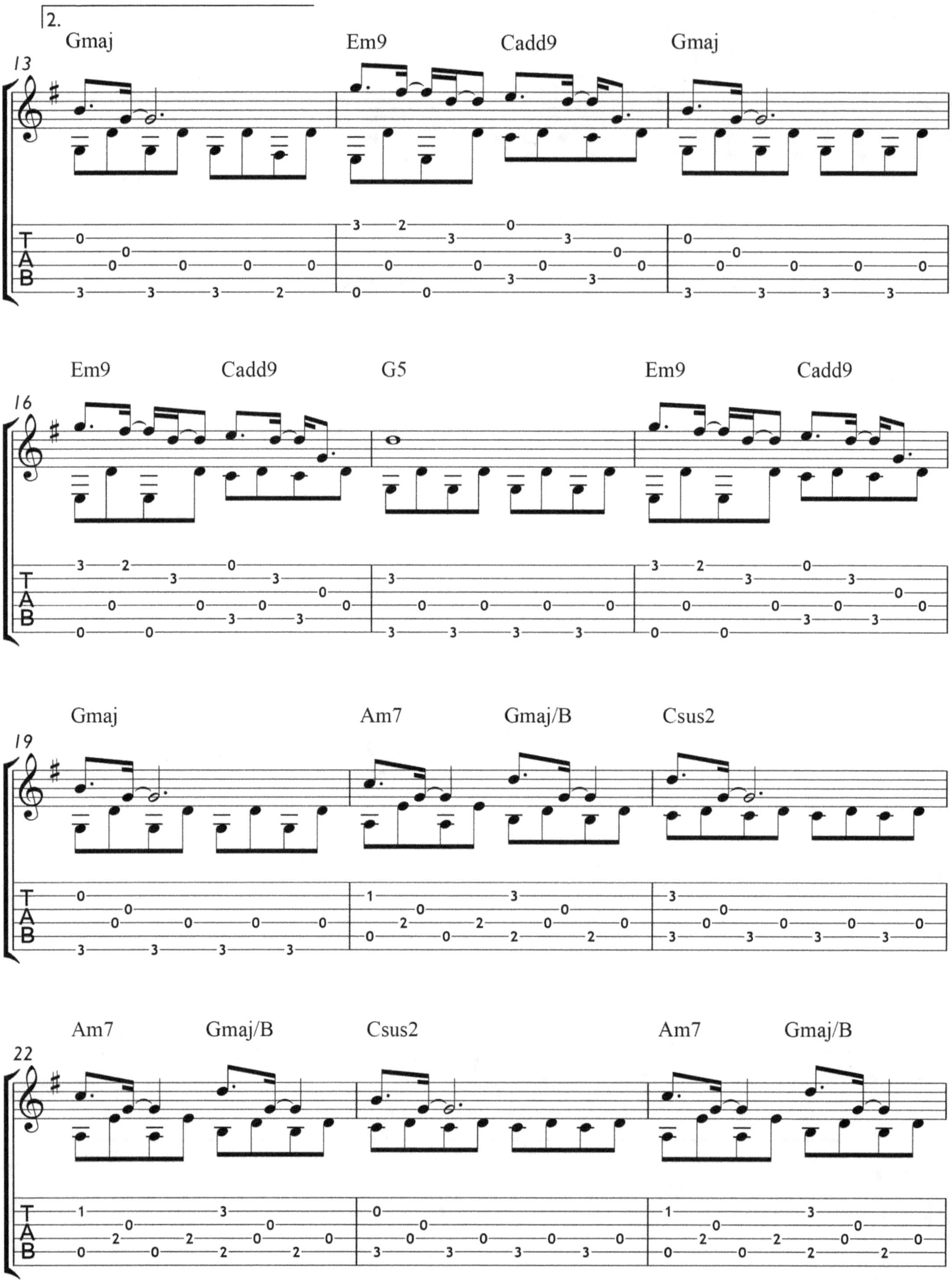
2.
Gmaj
Em9
Cadd9
Gmaj
13
Em9
Cadd9
G5
Em9
Cadd9
16
Gmaj
Am7
Gmaj/B
Csus2
19
Am7
Gmaj/B
Csus2
Am7
Gmaj/B
22

Gmaj D/F# Em Csus2 D6 G5
F6sus2 Cmaj Gmaj
F6sus2 Cmaj G5 F6sus2 Cmaj
Gmaj Dmaj/F# Em F6sus2 Gsus4 Gmaj

Track 3

There is a strong commercial side to many of today's modern Americana acts and the sound of the genre has well and truly entered the mainstream. Artists like The Civil Wars have a softer, melodic side that has brought them to the fore, and you'll even hear a somewhat diluted Americana sound in groups like Mumford and Sons.

This track demonstrates how an acoustic guitar can sit in a track, using many of the devices found in Americana, but rich, modern sounding chord voicings give it a contemporary feel. The opening section shows how many of today's artists use simple riff-based ideas in their writing. These are sparse parts that aren't too far away from their predecessors. While this modern sound is based on traditional chord progressions, it's the various extensions and alterations to the chords that provide a new sound within the genre.

From bar 17 you'll see chords that have a "bigger" more interesting sound than their standard major and minor counterparts. E.g. in bar 17, simply adding an open G string to a D major chord gives an extra level of character. Similarly, in bar 19 the addition of an open E string to a Bm7 takes that chord somewhere else altogether. When these chords are used in familiar progressions there is a sense of familiarity combined with an undeniable modernity.

The bulk of this track won't be too challenging to play. It's generally based around simple chord shapes and calls for clean, accurate strumming. When the fretting hand is comfortable with the shapes you'll be ready to go. This style can seem a world away from the early roots of Americana, but it shows how the genre has developed and adapted with each generation of songwriters. When you have learned this one, try re-writing the various strumming sections using your own chord shapes.

Example 7c

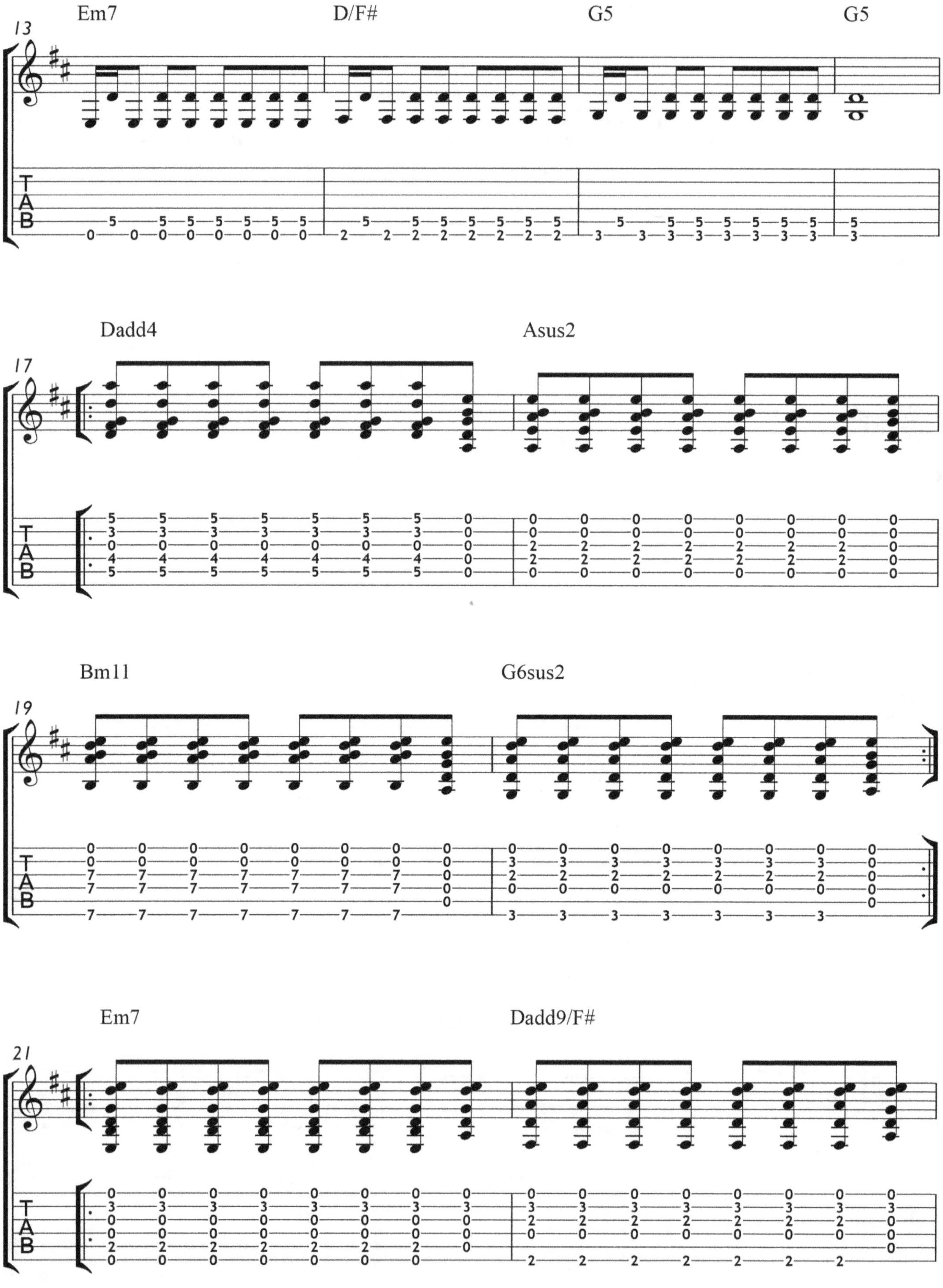
13
Em7
D/F#
G5
G5
17
Dadd4
Asus2
19
Bm11
G6sus2
21
Em7
Dadd9/F#

1.
2.
23
G6sus2
Asus4
26
Gmaj
D/F#
D
A/C#
G5
30
Gmaj
D/F#
D
D/F#
G5
34
D/F#
Bm7
Asus4
Gsus2
Gsus2
T
A
B

Track 4

This last track demonstrates how artists like Steve Earle and Bruce Springsteen have fused the traditional sounds of Americana –Bluegrass, Appalachian and Irish/Scottish – with modern, heavier sounding guitars and production. This track features a decidedly Appalachian style melody to begin with, and a mandolin – the traditional instrument of Bluegrass – is doubled with distorted guitars. This sound came to the fore in the 1980s thanks to tracks like Steve Earle's *Copperhead Road*, where a traditional aesthetic was fused with a modern, heavier sound. If you are new to playing melody lines like this, treat it as you would a solo or a long lick. Bluegrass and traditional players perform lines like this all day long, but getting the twists and turns of melodies and rhythms like this under the fingers can take some work.

We are using just the E Natural Minor scale here (E, F#, G, A, B, C, D) but the rhythms, melody and use of unisons – the same note played twice in different places (e.g. fret five of string 2 followed by the open 1st string) – give it that more traditional sound.

The traditional sound is contrasted with heavy, embellished chords which give way to a quite detailed rhythm part from bar 13. This melodic approach is another way of creating rhythmic parts which outline the underlying progression without just playing the chords. Again, we are using the E Natural Minor scale to create the ideas here.

The solo in this track starts at bar 21 and shows a useful approach for soloing in this genre – playing a moving melody line against an open string in order to thicken the sound. The solo is based around the E Minor Pentatonic scale (E, G, A, B, D), but instead of being played in a box shape it moves up string 2 with the open 1st string acting as a drone against it. This is a useful way of playing with some restraint as you have to think more about what you are doing, and the linear/vertical movement encourages you to slow down.

The solo concludes in the open position. Remember, it's well worth getting to grips with how things work down here, as so much of Americana guitar is based around open position playing.

Example 7d

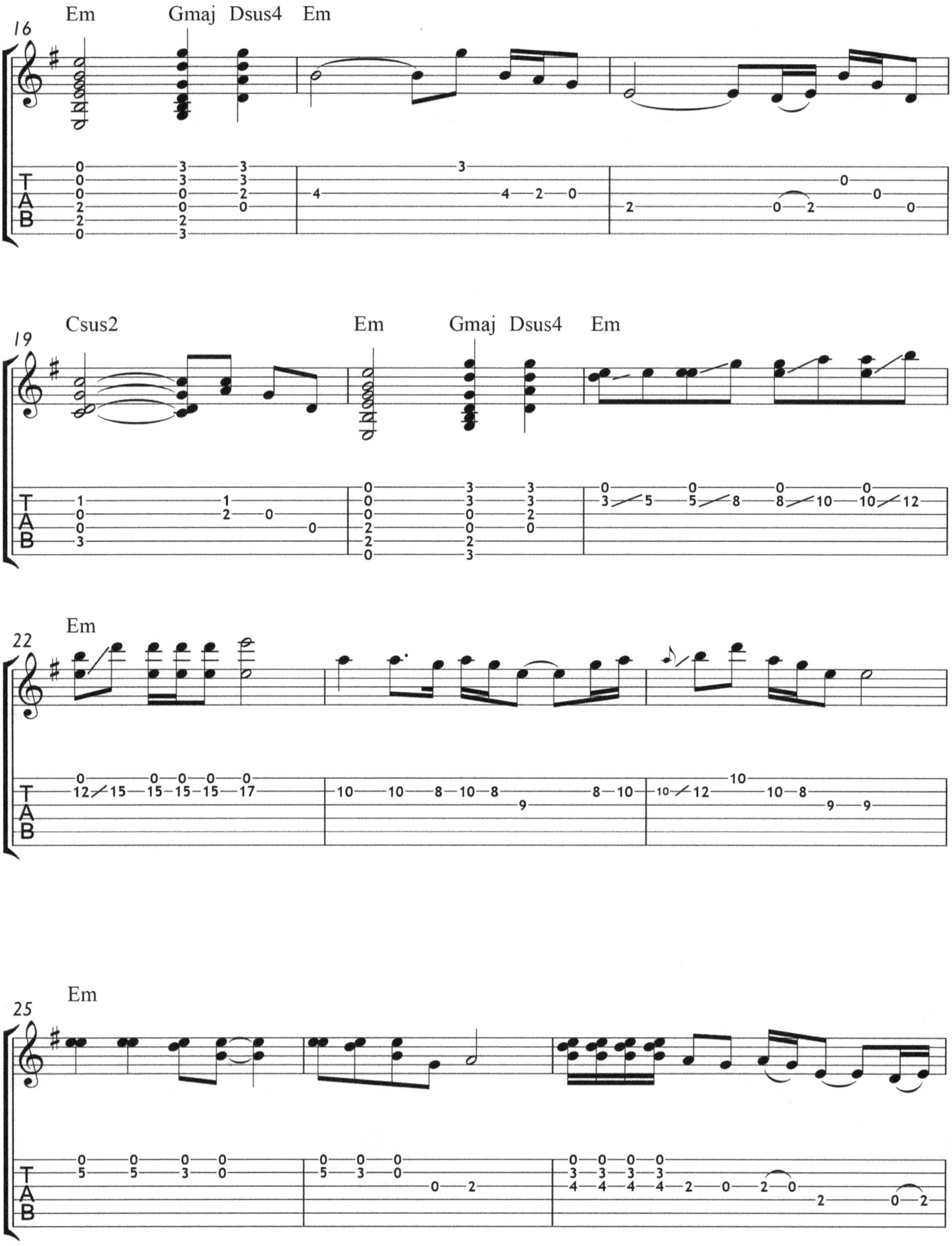
16
Em
Gmaj
Dsus4
Em
19
Csus2
Em
Gmaj
Dsus4
Em
22
Em
25
Em

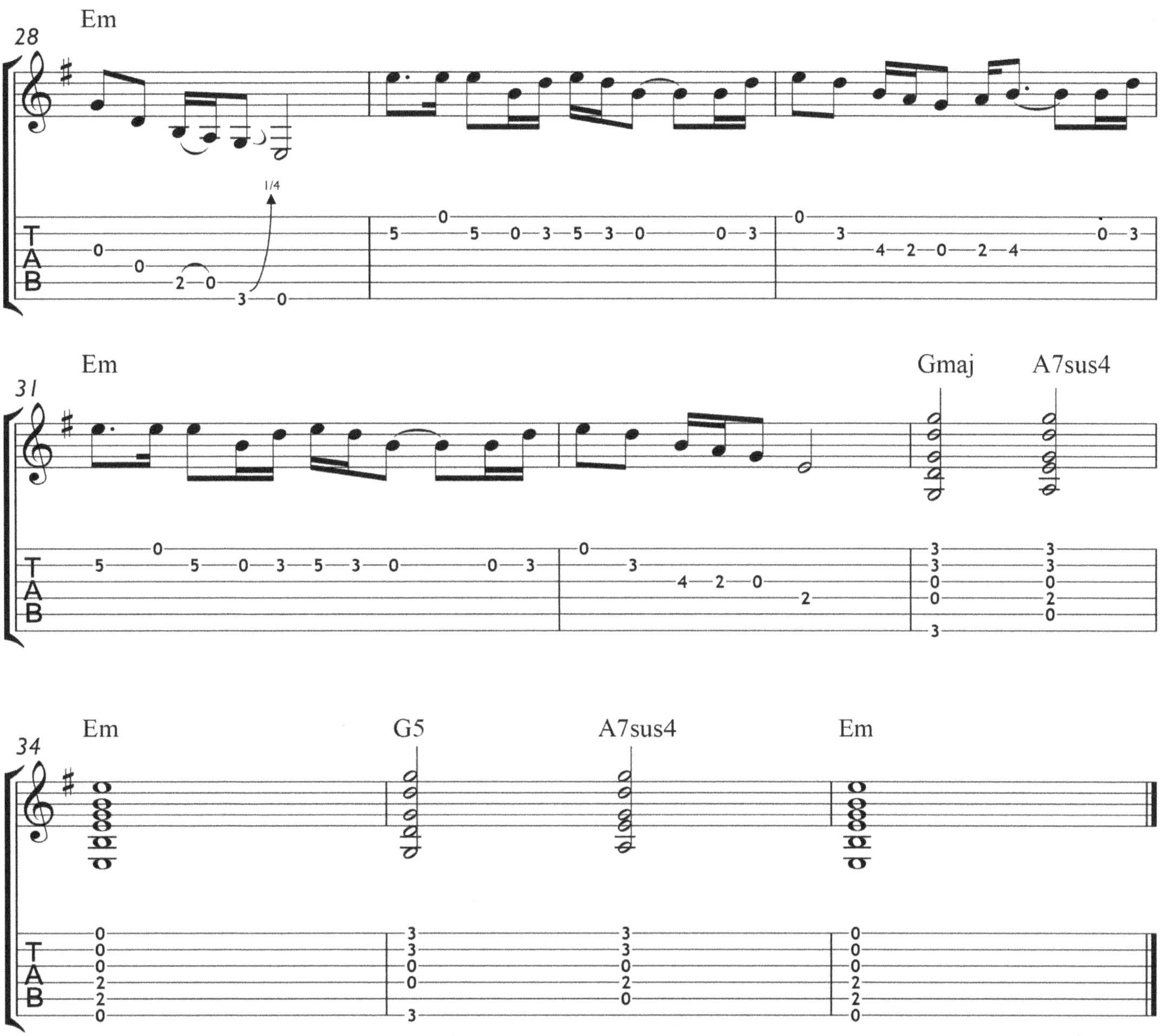
28
Em
1/4
31
Em
Gmaj
A7sus4
34
Em
G5
A7sus4
Em

Conclusion

As you'll have seen from this book, Americana is a huge genre that is a crucial part of America's musical history. From the early days of Bluegrass and Appalachian music through to today's modern Country, it is a genre that has a long heritage, shaped by many artists along the way.

It can be a difficult music to define, especially as the term used to describe it was coined only fairly recently, compared to its long history. But listen with an open mind, and begin your timeline from at least the 1940s, and you will get a sense of how expansive this genre is. Country, Bluegrass, Folk, Blues, Roots, Alt Rock, Outlaw Country… these are just some of the genres from which Americana draws, so you'll never be short of musical inspiration!

As a guitarist, I love the style as it encompasses so many musical worlds from acoustic to electric. What's more, there is so much to learn, from fingerpicking to Bluegrass melodies, new chords and song writing approaches.

Finally, remember that, as with all things Americana, the genre means different things to different people. Some will balk at the increasing commercialisation of the music, while others will embrace it. It means that, ultimately, you can define this music for yourself, taking inspiration from a wide range of sources; listening to areas that you love and seeing what roads Americana take you down.

Personally, I love it all, from the early days of Bill Monroe all the way through to today's Country superstars – it's all a source of inspiration, so get stealing some licks!

Acoustic Guitar Books From Fundamental Changes

Advanced Acoustic Fingerstyle Guitar

Beginner Acoustic Fingerstyle Guitar

Christmas Carols For Advanced Acoustic Guitar

Delta Blues Slide Guitar

Easy Christmas Carols For Guitar

How To Play Guitar – 3 in 1 Beginner Series

The Complete DADGAD Guitar Method

The Legends of Acoustic Guitar

Check them out here:

About the Author

"A world class guitarist, one of the finest of his generation."
–Martin Taylor MBE

"Will be one of the greatest guitarists this country has produced… a genius."
–Eric Roche

"That guitar sounds great in your hands!"
–Paul Reed Smith

"Super talented"
–Acoustic Magazine

"My friend Stuart Ryan is a fantabulous guitar player!"
–Jon Gomm

"My jaw dropped when you started playing!"
–Chris Difford (Squeeze)

Award winning musician Stuart Ryan is regarded as one of the UK's finest acoustic/electric guitarists. He began his professional career in 2002 when he was awarded *Guitarist Magazine's* Acoustic Guitarist of The Year and cemented his reputation with countless live appearances at concert halls, guitar festivals and clubs across the UK and Europe. A personal invitation by Martin Taylor MBE to appear at his Kirkmichael Guitar Festival in 2003 brought Stuart to the world stage and since then he has been busy as a concert guitarist, studio musician and author.

With a wide range of influences from rock guitarists to traditional blues and folk musicians and everything in between, his versatility has kept him busy and in demand. His solo guitar concerts take in everything from the haunting sounds of traditional music to the unbridled joy of African Kora alongside his own compositions and arrangements of well known pieces.

Follow Stuart's monthly tuition columns in *Guitar Techniques* and *Guitarist Acoustic* magazines. Discover more at **https://www.stuartryanmusic.com**